THE
BOOK
OF
LEADER

A TESTAMENT TO
THE ART OF LEADERSHIP

Jeff Pasquale

Contents

*For my sisters, Linda Pasquale and
Lauren Pasquale;
and my brothers, Richard (Rick) Pasquale
and Gerald (Jerry) Pasquale.
With love and respect.*

INTRODUCTION

Leadership is a never-ending process that involves discovery, wisdom, enjoyment, and balance.

While there are no strategies or tactics in this book, there are reflections, perspectives, and solid advice to help you grow in wisdom and in ways of relating—which are two of the biggest challenges leaders face today.

Leadership is an ideal that we must constantly strive for. Leadership is a lot like Zen—the moment you think you've got it figured out is when you're usually furthest away from it. In other words, leadership is something we aspire to, not something we occupy.

Each chapter in this book contains a universal truth that involves a leader's character, intentions, and level of caring. By reflecting on each of these concepts, and approaching them with patience, you'll find your definition of leadership changing for the better.

ONE

Leadership is an experience, not a destination.

The leadership experience is a conscious recognition that our intention is to be a leader, and we manifest this intention through our daily actions. Nothing more, nothing less.

If you pay more attention to that recognition versus the intention to lead, you become self-conscious. When acting self-consciously, you may end up doing and saying things that are far away from your original intention to lead.

Because of the endless nature of leadership, it can never be a destination.

There will always be the next decision, the next action, and the next communication. One cannot simply arrive at leadership. You may visit it from time to time, but you must always intend to come back... and you get back through your actions.

Be the leader you intend. Let go of where *you* want to go.

TWO

Leadership is an essential part of life; without it, people flounder. Not because we are incapable or helpless, but because we continually learn from watching and listening to others.

We all need higher ideals, standards, and worthy traits to aspire to. Leaders who lead through action, without preaching, tend to have a bigger positive impact on others.

Sometimes we take our leadership role for granted, and we forget that people are watching, noticing, commenting, or making unconscious decisions about how they should lead their lives based on what *we* do or don't do.

Conscious leadership is important, but it's just as important to not let it spill over into self-consciousness, when the ego takes over.

To be realistic, *conscious leadership* is a nice phrase with great intentions, but it's hardly the answer. Remembering that a leader simply sets direction, supports those she leads, and makes the occasional decision is enough to keep you out of trouble.

It's better to just remain conscious of the importance of leadership by actively looking for leadership in action — in others, not yourself.

When you look for leadership in action (in others), you are forcing yourself to look for the good in people, without judgment, and filtering out or ignoring the bad. Again, it's about them; not you. The key is to eliminate judgment.

THREE

A leader never needs to say, "I am the leader." Instead, he goes about his days being authentic and consistent, and living (and leading) simply.

Be honest, no one likes a person who goes around saying, "I'm in charge." It's lame, conceited, and brutish. It also conveys how powerless you actually feel. When people are not sure of themselves, they look for ways to amplify those areas they feel weakest in. Call it overcompensating.

The ideal way of leadership is also the most challenging. After all, who can possibly be authentic, consistent, and simplicity-minded in this hyper-competitive age?

The answer is very few of us, but that absolutely does not let us off the hook for not aiming high. Strive to set deliberately high standards because the people you lead need a role model.

People want leadership, Mr. President, and in the absence of genuine leadership, they'll listen to anyone who steps up to the microphone.
— from the movie *An American President*

The subtlety of the subject should not be missed. Most people will know that you're in charge (or that you are responsible for the outcome), so uttering the words *I'm in charge* is needless... unless you are trying to convince yourself.

FOUR

A leader knows more than she realizes. But if she ever starts believing that she knows more than others, the opposite may become true.

We are all good at fooling ourselves. Sometimes we'll actually lie to ourselves. What's worse is we tend to believe our own stories. (That's part of being human.)

A good leader catches the self-deception and corrects it.

She then goes one step further and doesn't beat herself up over what she has done, but rather acknowledges her misstep and goes back to leading.

The same holds true when we pass judgment. A leader who believes she is seldom wrong or that she is a better than someone else is straying from the true essence of leadership.

The truth is that each of us has a different reality and perspective, and who is to say which one is true, which one is real or which one is closer to the truth?

The good leader strives for balance; she pushes away judgments when they crop up, and seeks to understand before acting.

FIVE

A leader doesn't judge—he discerns. Is it just? Is it fair? Is it mutually beneficial? These are questions a leader must ask himself as a habit.

So much of what we do each day is done unconsciously. We have learned so many automatic responses that we don't even realize they are automatic.

The hardest part about leading (and living) is doing so without judgment. So often, we jump to a conclusion or make a decision based on our biases or prejudgments about a situation, a person, or an organization.

Sometimes we're correct in feeling apprehension, especially if we have been hurt before. But if it is an automatic response, then it's wise to momentarily reconsider our decision.

If a leader has trained well, he will have programmed himself to automatically look for opportunities that are fair and beneficial to all. And that training comes with practice.

SIX

A leader avoids nothing. He will quickly confront issues and problems, both large and small, to prevent those he leads from experiencing problems or falling into a state of confusion or concern.

A leader is responsible. He takes responsibility for outcomes. He doesn't jump from one thing to another, leaving a wake of questions behind him. He manages and leads.

Leaders who avoid issues are generally considered ineffective. But what isn't addressed is who gets hurt as a result of the leader's avoidance. Taking responsibility for outcomes means proactively taking ownership of the problem that arises, when it arises. Not waiting for the issue to find you, but taking the steps to face it.

Take stock in the power you have when you confront even the smallest issue. By doing so, you reassure those you lead that you really do care, and that you really are in charge.

SEVEN

A leader intends mastery with everything she does. Mastery takes many forms. A good leader is a master storyteller, a master relationship-builder, and a master manager.

This may sound like a leader needs to be the proverbial triple threat, and in some ways that's true. But when broken down into component parts, each role is really quite simple:

As a *storyteller*, the leader expresses her vision of the future (what her team or company could/should be). As a *relationship-builder*, she shows others how to get things done through cooperation versus confrontation. And as a *manager*, she models efficiency and good stewardship.

These three roles are essential components to the mastery of leadership. None work so cohesively together.

Remember that leadership is a work in progress. We're never quite there; we're always learning and we're always being tested. Consider your role as a leader to be your own private, never-ending leadership training school.

Leadership lessons occur throughout our day, and each one is an opportunity for us to get one step closer to mastery.

EIGHT

Leadership is about cooperation, accountability, and solutions. It's never about blaming.

A leader who faults someone else (another department, company, or political party) for a situation is not leading—he's shifting responsibility.

Anyone can say: *"It's not my fault."* A leader takes responsibility for the situation, good or bad.

Accusing and blaming are the traits of someone who does not have a solution. When a leader wants to cooperate, attempts to find common ground, and consistently offers innovative solutions, it is easier to see who is and who isn't participating.

The world is tough, but a leader can counter by relentlessly working to bring people together.

Leaders don't need to point out problems or blame. They need to bring solutions.

NINE

A leader is not afraid to display love; it comes in many forms.

Love is evidenced by how much someone cares. This caring comes from a deep, unadulterated concern for the people around you and those you lead.

Some might consider this the soft side of leadership when in fact it's a sign of strength, because you are comfortable with showing your emotions (without drama). You know how to convey a feeling, express a thought, or take action in a manner that is decorous, yet heartfelt.

Leaders who wear a façade of sternness usually do so in order to convey power or strength. People sometimes wear this mask to hide their perceived fears or shortcomings. Their mantra is: "*A good offense is a great defense.*"

Individuals who are not afraid to display love take their leadership roles (and their lives) seriously. They recognize that they have a responsibility to leave things better than they found them. This expression of caring has the power to unify, solidify, and amplify a team's sense of worth and accomplishment.

Possessing a strong sense of love and caring for those you lead helps your team grow into something better.

TEN

A good leader knows how to avoid getting pulled into confrontations that have no relevance to the matters at hand.

There is a proper time and place for confrontations. A negative confrontation usually occurs when two contrasting viewpoints meet and emotion is involved. That meeting can be disruptive, if not hurtful.

It's up to the leader to take the high road and not get sucked into allowing a confrontation to become personal.

Confrontations are not always bad. A leader knows when it's time to deal with a challenging issue, or if it's better to let it go for a later time. (That's not avoidance; that's good leadership.)

The good leader consciously chooses when it's time to take a stand for something that must be dealt with for the good of all concerned.

Some leaders make careers out of confrontations. Good leaders choose confrontations wisely and center their careers on leading.

ELEVEN

A leader recognizes that she is being watched.

This is not about the self-conscious thought of a conceited person, but the thoughtful response and acknowledgement of a person who understands human nature.

The good leader stays focused on what she needs to do, but remains mindful of those watching. She does this out of concern for those she leads, wanting only to ensure that they understand both her intentions as well as her actions.

The fact that she is the leader induces people to automatically, almost unconsciously, watch what she does. And after watching comes the judgments: *Is she kind? Is she considerate? Is she wise in her decisions? Can she be trusted? Does she honor those not present by never speaking badly about them?*

These questions and judgments add up, and they explain how people perceive their leader.

TWELVE

Leading is always a work in progress.

This news should not be discouraging. It's simply a reminder not to fall prey to ego—that little voice in our heads that's constantly judging, and insidiously trying to coax us into believing we're better or smarter than everyone else.

Believing that you've figured out the secrets to leadership success is a little like thinking you've figured out the secret to happiness; it's a mirage.

Leadership will always be a work in progress because we are always changing, and so is everything around us. How we perceive, respond, or anticipate events will change from day to day. Count on it.

We are measured by our last success. And then we start over.

THIRTEEN

A good leader knows that if everything matters, then few things get done.

Leadership requires focus and follow-through; without them, little is accomplished. It's hard to stay focused when you're paying attention to everything.

A leader knows that determining what to work on next is a matter of prioritization and discernment. Although popular opinion may cry out for one action, another priority may need to be managed first.

While her actions may cause her to feel like the loneliest person in town, a leader knows that in the long run, results are more important than opinions.

Everything matters, yes, but everything is not important.

FOURTEEN

A leader seeks to build trust and respect in every relationship. He does this by going first.

A good leader knows that not everyone will respond with the same level of trust and respect, but he knows that he must model the behavior he wishes to see in those around him.

This is a sound strategy for great leadership in action.

A first response to someone who acts disrespectfully or in an untrustworthy manner might be met with judgment or scorn. A leader knows that these feelings do not inspire people to change for the better. A leader knows it is better to respond with compassion.

This doesn't mean people who act this way should not be held accountable—but it's just not worth a leader's time and energy to be judgmental or scornful.

Trust and respect are essential in every relationship, no matter how casual. A leader considers solid relationships the building blocks of greater things.

FIFTEEN

Leadership is never static. It is in constant motion.

There will be times when your leadership is hyperactive and other times when it's in slow motion. One thing is for certain—leadership is always in action.

This is because a leader intends forward motion. Unless total disengagement is the choice we make (as with meditation), the result of inaction tends to be thought, which means if we're not doing, then we're probably thinking...and thinking doesn't get things done.

A good leader knows the difference between thinking things through and being paralyzed in thought. Sometimes there is a fine line between the two, and it's up the leader to know where that line is.

Thinking is important, plans are important, but action is more important.

SIXTEEN

A leader has an eye for the past, another for the present, and the third for the future.

She focuses mostly on the present (the center of activity), but remains mindful of where she came from (the past), and where she intends to go (the future).

The past is a leader's history, to learn and to grow from. A good leader knows the past should not be dwelled upon for very long, but it is a valuable point of reference.

The future is where she intends to take things. She looks ahead consistently to ensure that she and those she leads are going in the right direction.

A leader knows that the present is *right now*. Things are always happening at the center. She knows the positive impact she can have on things in the moment.

SEVENTEEN

Leadership is about the example you set, and the results your team achieves.

Each day, feelings of frustration or indifference can surface and cause a leader to become ineffective. At those times it is especially important for the leader to remind herself exactly what it is she wants to accomplish in order to not lose momentum.

She doesn't get angry or lose her temper; she regroups and gets on with her work. A good leader models the behavior she wishes to see in those she leads. She looks for opportunities to celebrate often.

EIGHTEEN

A leader knows the importance of silence.

A good leader knows when it's time to listen and when it's time to speak. They are mutually exclusive.

Silencing the brain is also important. Learning how to quiet the mind allows for thoughts, feelings, and inklings to occur. Instead of listening with the intention to reply, hear with the intention to understand. It is a learned trait, one that is especially needed in this media era of refutation and rebuttal.

When a person (a leader or otherwise) consistently interrupts, it is clear he is not completely listening. People in general want to be heard by their leader, to simply be heard.

Silence is a powerful tool a leader can and should use throughout her day. It gives her time to think and time to really hear what's going on.

NINETEEN

A leader knows that she must be equal parts competent manager and competent leader.

While the two skills/attributes are sometimes used interchangeably, they are not the same.

Management involves logic; leadership requires heart. Both are essential elements to good business.

Management is about the business; leadership is about people. The good manager is mindful of the business's basics — budgets, timelines, and procedures. Leadership is about goals, empowerment, and morale.

It's easy for a manager to get caught up in the details of managing and ignore people. Overzealous as managers are about production and profit, it is not usually out of maliciousness. They have simply gotten caught up in the details.

The good manager knows when it's time to log off of the computer and talk to her people as the leader.

TWENTY

A leader dances well.

When an awkward or tense situation occurs, it should not stop a leader from moving forward. She recovers quickly, deals with the situation, and gets back to what she was doing.

Too often in today's culture, an awkward situation brings out the façade of coolness in a leader, or worse, ignorance. We have somehow learned how to avoid issues and continue behaving as if nothing is wrong.

This is an admirable trait if you intend to prevent people from panicking. But if the intention is to remain composed (fake it until you can figure things out because you don't want to look bad), you're not dancing. You're deceiving.

There is nothing wrong with keeping your composure in an uncomfortable situation. The problem arises when a leader deliberately misrepresents what she knows in order to appear knowledgeable.

TWENTY-ONE

A leader is comfortable saying the words *"I don't know."* He knows this is not a sign of weakness, but a sign of honesty.

The leader is just as comfortable hearing others say those same words to him. He knows it is an opportunity for both parties to act quickly and find out the answer so that it can be relayed back as quickly as possible.

The leader who says, "I don't know, let me find out and get back to you," (and doesn't) isn't leading. He's pretending to lead. In time, this type of deceptive leadership will be uncovered, and he will quickly find himself disrespected by those being led.

The good leader also knows there is power behind the words *I don't know* AND *let me find out*.

TWENTY-TWO

The leader is able to see greatness in people. She does this by taking the time to get to know people and hearing their stories.

The good leader makes the effort to seek and find greatness in others. She believes that people are inherently good; but she also has the wisdom to know that sometimes this goodness is overshadowed by greed, selfishness, and bias.

Being able to see through the flaws in others and recognize the good qualities enables her to play off of their strengths while remaining aware of their weaknesses. The leader helps people see the good in themselves that they may have forgotten.

TWENTY-THREE

There's always a bigger vision (or goal) to consider when leading. But the good leader knows that the only thing she can really work on is what's right in front of her.

While this may sound obvious, it's really about patience and persistence. It also addresses how a leader can masterfully blend the short-term needs of the people she leads with the long-term needs of those who benefit from everyone's work.

Sometimes the simplest task can have the biggest impact on a long-term goal. A good leader knows that if she consistently reminds everyone of the importance of their one big goal, even though it's only in a few words, that those words will carry her team to long-term success.

TWENTY-FOUR

A leader values his relationships by making the effort to stay in contact, recognizing accomplishments, and offering support.

A good leader knows the long-term benefits of supporting his employees and recognizing good work. Some leaders are hesitant to do either for fear of looking weak. A leader must always be guided by what he believes to be right.

Good relationships can allow things to happen more quickly. Great relationships are built on trust and respect, and they are nurtured by support, recognition, and regular contact.

TWENTY-FIVE

A leader knows the importance of flexibility.

She knows that most goals do not go according to plan, and that unexpected delays or situations can arise at any time. A leader can bend with the situation but never lose sight of her target.

There will be times when flexibility is not an option, and tenacity and fortitude will be required. When backed against the wall, so to speak, a good leader will never resort to arrogance or hostility to get her way.

Like water wearing down a rock, the leader knows that time and persistence will pay off if she remains vigilant to the task at hand.

The good leader knows there is strength in flexibility, and that inflexibility can become a weight that pulls her down, and the people she is leading.

TWENTY-SIX

A good leader is not swayed or influenced by power or opulence; she sees them for what they are—fleeting prizes that are nice to have, but are not the true components of happiness or success.

This neutrality allows a leader to be impartial and fair, without being affected by the abundance of excess.

The leader knows that her intention is to lead, not to accumulate. She believes that what you gain is sometimes more problematic than what you lose. She knows that the real treasures in life are her family, friends, and the goodness that she sees in her surroundings.

TWENTY-SEVEN

A leader values *teamwork* as an essential component of good leadership.

Teamwork cannot exist without a good leader. It is simply not possible. Teamwork cannot be forced and manipulated. Teamwork stems from the trust and respect that people on the team have for the leader, and for each other.

The good leader knows how to entrust her team to the pursuit and accomplishment of worthy goals. She knows that they know when she is being disingenuous or self-serving, so she chooses to go about her days being of service and being supportive to her team.

TWENTY-EIGHT

A leader knows that she need not be the sole source of inspiration for her organization.

Sometimes leaders feel pressure to be the number one cheerleader and morale booster for their organization.

This pressure is false and unnecessary.

A good leader never feels or views her cheerleading as an external pressure because her desire to fulfill the role comes from within.

Although she is responsible for the company's morale, she does not carry that responsibility on her back. She simply identifies other highly visible and competent motivators with whom she can share the role.

TWENTY-NINE

A leader recognizes that everyone is a leader, and therefore he listens closely to what people have to say.

He is not influenced by those who are strong-willed. Yet he is keenly aware of silence. Those who say the least are the ones he listens to most closely, while the louder ones say too much. In the gap, the leader knows the wisdom of the team will emerge.

In the busy culture that a leader now exists in, it takes endless practice to listen to everyone as though they are leaders, too.

THIRTY

A leader knows how to enjoy life. She knows that worrying seldom solves problems and has the ability to cripple innovation, passion, and inspiration.

Fun may seem like a rare feeling for a leader, but it's the wise leader who knows that life and leading should have an element of enjoyment; otherwise, what's the point?

The good leader knows that choosing lightheartedness goes a long way towards introducing and instilling fun or enjoyment into the things she does. This feeling must be genuine, not forced, and it must be shared with others, not kept in a closet for private consumption.

THIRTY-ONE

A leader knows that sometimes he is his own biggest obstacle.

We sometimes make the problem bigger than it really is.

At the same time, the good leader resists imposing his will upon the people he leads. While there will be times when he feels especially strong about a problem his team is up against, he has learned how and when to back off and let those he leads take responsibility.

In this action of sharing power, the leader is acting selflessly by not allowing his will to become an obstacle to himself or others.

THIRTY-TWO

A leader knows that effective management is as important as effective leadership. There is balance to everything in life; too much of one creates a deficiency of another.

It has been said that you manage things and you lead people. The amount of time and the level of involvement she allots for each activity is evidence of a good leader.

The leader knows the importance of balance, that there is a time to speak and a time to listen, a time to think and a time for action, a time for nurturing and a time for counseling.

THIRTY-THREE

A leader knows the importance of a handwritten note to recognize or acknowledge the important and not-so-important things she notices.

Yes, writing by hand is a slowly dying habit, but they will probably be saying this fifty years from now, so don't give up just yet.

While a personal note can convey thanks, appreciation, or concern, the good leader knows that a handwritten note says, "*I care*."

Though it takes extra time to craft and create, the handwritten note is a powerful way to show the importance of your feelings and concerns. It's a proven fact that a handwritten note, regardless of its content, will be saved by the recipient far longer than an email or typed correspondence.

THIRTY-FOUR

A leader knows how to speak from her head and from her heart so that a balanced message is sent and received.

A good leader doesn't need a speech writer to put words in her mouth. When a leader speaks only from the head, logic and statistics come out, and the human element is kept to a minimum, which alienates people.

When a leader speaks primarily from the heart, emotion dominates, and though the message may resonate with people, they are left wondering how things will get done.

The blend of head and heart makes a leader more human to those she leads.

THIRTY-FIVE

A leader knows that simply acting like a leader does not make him a leader.

A good leader is knowledgeable about his strengths and his faults. He knows there is power in just being himself. He drops pretenses and façades, and lets his authentic self be seen by others.

The wise leader knows that it is easier to be authentic and hold on to lofty goals than to act sternly and force accomplishments to happen.

THIRTY-SIX

A good leader knows that being a leader can sometimes be a lonely position.

A leader knows that she will experience the ups and downs of leadership, which sometimes include moments of cloudiness or moments of clarity.

Leadership can be lonely when the weight of responsibility falls on one set of shoulders.

But the leader knows she is a leader by choice.

While this doesn't make it any easier, there are four things she does to properly recover after a bad experience:

She gives herself five minutes to feel bad...

...she recharges her batteries...

...she refocuses her attention...

...And then she gets up and gets back to work.

THIRTY-SEVEN

A leader knows that her ability to lead can be measured by how well things run while she's away.

Though this sounds harsh, it is critical that things continue to move forward with or without the leader's presence, otherwise she is the one doing all of the work, which isn't leadership.

Lao Tzu's verse on leadership rings true here: "...*at the end of the day, the people say, 'We did it ourselves.'*"

THIRTY-EIGHT

A leader knows that the best way to give and receive trust is to be trustworthy. Sometimes trust is mistaken for gallantry or civility. Unfortunately, someone who is civil can also be untrustworthy.

A good leader knows how to identify trustworthy persons. He does this not by testing people but by observing their actions and looking for consistency. Does that person do what he says he'll do, on time and as promised?

The leader knows that he needs to do the same, and be consistent in word and deed.

THIRTY-NINE

A leader is not afraid when the dull roar of silence surrounds her. Whether in dialogue with a group of people or in a serious one-on one-conversation, a leader is able to fully embrace silence for what it is...an opportunity to pause and gain clarity.

This particular kind of silence is not generated by the leader but by the world around her. There will be times when a pause in conversation occurs and a leader may feel compelled to fill that space with words rather than letting the silence be.

A good leader recognizes that a brief silence is as powerful as the most inspirational words she can say. She therefore welcomes and holds on tightly to those short periods of silence.

FORTY

A leader consistently appreciates the gifts she has around her – her friends, coworkers, and associates, as well as her health, and the many blessings she has in her life.

She not only appreciated these gifts, she acknowledges them, too. The good leader recognizes how quickly time flies, and that it is vitally important to convey all feelings of gratitude as soon as they are felt. This is not a race that a leader tries to win, but a race that is never-ending because she never knows when circumstances will change and the opportunity to say *thank you* is gone.

This sense of urgency drives a leader to be on the lookout for things to appreciate and recognize. She has learned that the more she appreciates, the more gifts she has.

FORTY-ONE

A leader knows that if she interferes too much with the work of others that their work can veer off course due to distraction.

It is hard for everyone (not just the leader) to let other people be responsible to their own work. A good leader knows when the time is right to check up on progress or if it's necessary to remind people of the deadline that's looming. It's about discernment and respect.

A leader knows that if she's done her job well, she has the right people in the right positions to get the job done. At that point she merely needs to trust in her judgment and trust in her team's capability and sense of responsibility.

FORTY-TWO

A leader knows when it's time to stop pushing and to let things happen. Pushing, forcing, cajoling, and leveraging are all tactics. The leader knows that if nothing happens unless he presses, then something is missing in the equation.

A good leader knows that true power may appear weak at first and that great wisdom may initially appear childish. He has the patience to give things time, to let them happen. He knows that if a strong foundation has been laid, with a vision, plans, and correct information, things can be accomplished with little involvement from him.

Practicing patience is never-ending; it requires trust on the leader's part that those he leads will do what is expected of them without having to push or threaten.

FORTY-THREE

A leader recognizes the importance of empathy, and he relies on it to keep him in touch with the people he leads.

With leadership, it's easy to feel disconnected from people. The responsibilities, the decisions, and the schedule can wear you down. A good leader takes the time to not only listen to others but to attempt to feel what it's like to be in their shoes.

FORTY-FOUR

A leader knows that the conflicts and disagreements that she has with others will ultimately hurt those she leads.

This does not mean she is afraid to confront or disagree. She doesn't personalize these situations, allowing things to escalate to the point when there is a personal battle that must be won.

When conflict is necessary, the leader is not afraid to defend her boundaries or say what needs to be said. She steps over or avoids nothing.

It takes courage for a leader to not speak up when everyone else feels it is necessary to meet force head on. A good leader knows that force and skillful words are not the only means to succeed in the face of conflict.

Sometimes all that is required of a leader is to hear or see the conflict, and then continue moving in the intended direction she wants her team to go.

FORTY-FIVE

A good leader has learned the art of balancing firmness, compassion, and accountability with humility. A leader is consistent in her behaviors and her values.

There are some leaders who feel they must play the part and act shrewd and stern. This behavior may get results, but people will eventually resent the coercion.

Leadership means being all things to all people, but it applies mostly to how a person leads. If the leader is firm, compassionate, responsible, and empathetic, she has a greater chance of reaching a larger number of people with her leadership.

Consistency of behavior and values is essential to good leadership. They must be practiced on a daily basis.

FORTY-SIX

A leader believes that by serving the needs of others, he himself will be fulfilled.

It can be difficult to be virtuous and selfless in a leadership position, but these are essential qualities a leader must possess if he is to be successful in his endeavors.

This does not mean that a leader must sacrifice or even suffer in the execution of his duties; it simply means that he considers others first in order to ensure that his ego is not driving the bus.

FORTY-SEVEN

A leader leaves ample time and space in her day just to think.

Thinking is important, and usually in the busy life of a leader, thinking is a luxury, which is why a good leader actively looks for the time.

The good leader knows that too much thinking and less action will nullify her ability to lead, so she makes sure she is attentive to the delicate balance, ensuring that action always wins.

FORTY-EIGHT

A leader thinks and acts long-term. He knows that he will not be the leader forever; therefore he leads with both long-term and short-term intentions.

A wise leader doesn't leap at the short-term win to enjoy victory; he knows that successive leaders will either have to fix or build upon what he has started.

The good leader chooses long-term action that will benefit those living today as well as their descendants.

FORTY-NINE

A leader embraces simplicity as a way of life and as a way of leading. This ensures that as many people as possible will understand what a leader is doing, or is intending to do.

Sometimes a culture is mired in excess: too many words, too many slogans, too many agendas, and too many mixed messages, which is deliberate of a leader with bad intentions. Complexity ensures that the real truth won't be discovered, thereby assuring a longer tenure.

A good leader sticks to simple messages with simple intentions. This way things can be accomplished more quickly and with less confusion, and the people

being led will see the intention and the
desired result.

FIFTY

A leader does not succumb to the emotional pressures and fads of the day.

Her decisions are based on the needs of the organization and its customers. There may be times when the latest trend or fad is a perfect fit for her organization, and it will be adopted because it fits...period.

There may also be issues that call for expediency on the leader's part, not because of something she wants, but because those she leads feel that it is important for her to support and promote for their joint success.

Expediency is distinctively different from being overly compulsive or reactive.

FIFTY-ONE

A leader sees herself as a good steward.

She knows that she is entrusted to this role for but a short time and treats this opportunity as a blessing.

While leadership is a responsibility, and a serious one, a good leader also believes that it is an opportunity and a privilege.

FIFTY-TWO

A good leader firmly believes that her primary role is to provide support.

While all of the previous steps are important, the leader who fully supports her people knows that support translates into a culture of confidence and excellence in everyone's minds.

Being of service and being supportive of those she leads not only models good leadership, but also sows the seeds for other good leaders to emerge.

THE END IS
THE BEGINNING

Leadership is an ideal. It is something to work towards that inspires others. It cannot be faked, mimicked, or induced.

Leadership will always require a higher level of thinking regardless of time and circumstance. Things may change in the way leaders approach problems and create solutions, but the universal themes of service and support will always remain a priority in effective leadership.

Leadership is always a work in progress, and your role as leader will continuously change. But two key elements that will never change is your role to serve and to support those you lead—not the other way around.

If you can avoid this pitfall, and you proactively seek to provide service and support to those around you, you may find that leadership is actually easier than you think.

It can be that simple.

ACKNOWLEDGEMENTS

It is easy to occasionally take our leadership roles for granted. Not because we don't care, but because we allow ourselves to become so immersed in what we're doing that we begin leading by remote control. We begin making *efficient* leadership decisions instead of *effective* leadership decisions.

I wish to thank the following individuals for their distinctive and effective leadership styles, which I have admired and modeled over the years: Nat Nason, Greg Kissel, Matt Peace, Greg Behl, Kenyetta Haywood, Monte Lambert, Bill Bone, Rick Seymour, and Roy Assad.

My thanks, too, to my consistently supportive friends, advisors, and cheerleaders: Jim Sugarman, Monte Lambert, Bill Bone, Lew Pincus, Cal Miller, Nick Tamposi, and Missy Duffy.

A nod of appreciation to Tom Peters and Seth Godin-their work on the subjects of leadership, excellence, and creativity has been enlightening and inspiring.

Thanks, also, to Kammy Wood for her thoughtful and insightful editing, and to Sebastian, who designs books with care, consistency, and creativity.

Thanks, once again, to Maura and Vanessa for their support, inspiration, and love.

Jeff Pasquale is an Executive and Life Coach who works specifically in the areas of life, leadership, and legacy.

He is the author of:

The Magic Dance – *Do You Lead, Follow, or Get Out of the Way?*;

How BIG is Your Target – *The Power of Focus in a Cluttered World*;

Looking for SUNSHINE — *A Practical Guide for Dealing with Life's Challenges*;

Subway Life – *An Underground Guide to Balanced Living*;

Get That New Job – *Self-Coaching Steps That Work*; and

Coaching Leadership – *If Not You, Who?*

He lives in Boynton Beach, Florida.

More information about Jeff and additional tools can be found at:

www.JeffPasquale.com

NOTES:

NOTES:

NOTES:

NOTES: